LADDER OF HOURS

Poems 1969—2005

☾

Keith Althaus

AUSABLE PRESS
2005

Design and composition by Ausable Press
The type is Bembo with Bembo Titling.
Cover design by Rebecca Soderholm

Published by
AUSABLE PRESS
1026 Hurricane Road
Keene, NY 12942
www.ausablepress.org

Distributed to the trade by
CONSORTIUM BOOK SALES & DISTRIBUTION
1045 Westgate Drive
Saint Paul, MN 55114-1065
(651) 221-9035
(651) 221-0124 (fax)
(800) 283-3572 (orders)

The acknowledgments appear on page 175 and constititute a
continuation of the copyright page.

Library of Congress Cataloging-in-Publication Data

Althaus, Keith.
Ladder of hours : poems 1969—2005 / by Keith Althaus. —1st ed.
p. cm.
ISBN-13: 978-1-931337-27-4 (pbk. : alk. paper)
ISBN-10: 1-931337-27-6
I. Title.
PS3551.L777L33 2005
811'.54—dc22
2005014471

For my mother

ALSO BY KEITH ALTHAUS

Rival Heavens
Provincetown Arts Press, 1993

LADDER OF HOURS

CONTENTS

ON THIS SIDE

On this side
there are forests,
white in winter,
that turn in spring
a perishing green,
water that circles;
on its cloud-rain-sea cycle
tears are a step.
So are the lakes
that remember and forget
the sky all day.
There is the slow speed
of atoms in wood and steel,
and their racing in steam and breath.
On this side
we have bodies,   .
weightless at times,
at times stone.
On this side . . .
I could go on.
I could name everything.
But the names would soon
sound absurd, each like
the only word we know
in a foreign language,
and over there
nothing would hear anyway,
nothing sees.
On that side
it is darker than blindness,
and the silence is louder

than that which wakes us
suddenly, fallen asleep
to music or noise.

FIRST MEMORY

The taillights disappearing
into the black wood of the hill
mark the end of my reach,
the limit of my knowledge.
Before that there is nothing.
Sometimes I am awakened by the slamming
of brakes, or the jerky shifting of gears
going uphill, the clattering of an empty trolley
through a deserted, unlit intersection.
Sometimes I am filled with enormous sadness
for no reason, as a car veers off up ahead
or a city bus slows to make a turn farther
and farther behind me.

YOU DROPPED SOMETHING

You dropped something
off a bridge
then ran across the road
to watch it come out
the other side.
It never did.
You scan the surfaces of years
for any change:
the green marble of the deep
swirls with clouds and limbs,
birds and leaves swim
backwards in formation;
what you've lost
is buried on the bottom,
part of the river's salt,
one of its nameless
heavy things that moves in clouds
until it's caught by living nets.

Your brain is a factory of secrets,
now idle,
down to a watchman
making the rounds
with a swinging clock,
tunneling back
to a light bent
over a desk.

Whose footsteps are those
heartbeats behind you?
Whose hand lies asleep in yours
as in a glove?

LADDER OF HOURS

A ladder of hours
leads to the dark.
Midnight's tower
looks down on
where you stood
at noon, poised
on a rung,
wondering
what is this room
that stands outside,
in pure light,
even as the ladder
curves in space
to meet itself,
become a treadmill,
whose blurring bars create
a see-through wall,
on the other side of which,
the room endures, and waits,
though moonlit now.

MAY 19, 2003

One day no one
reading this date
will have lived then:
this morning when
the cherry is in bloom,
and the dog lounges
by the door not anxious
to come in, and bees
bounce limb to limb,
and an oriole visits
from the long cloudless blue
that stands behind, above it all.
Explanation is unnecessary,
just someone to describe
its routine beauty,
the ordinary day, nothing special,
one of many, exceptional only
as the breath you catch again
having lost it.

IN TRAFFIC

These swirling forms,
fleeting, gone—
exhaust of a cold engine
turning onto the highway,
accelerated lives of ghosts,
breaths torn to shreds,
the unsaid returning
to the alphabet.
More cars merge and exit;
other chimneys smudge the sky
with the same mistakes,
other stands of trees
this lonely race past,
exposing fences underneath,
and nests up high, and all of this
continues, after you've driven by
and are fast asleep, like music
too briefly heard to name.

CZESLAW MILOSZ

"The optimistic occupation of studying languages. An etymological dictionary of the Russian language, four volumes of Greek, Karlowicz's and Linde's dictionaries of Polish, *Modern Lithuanian,* Bruckner's etymological dictionary of Polish, a dictionary of Indo–European roots in English. An optimistic occupation because it implies a goal, a utility that runs counter to common sense. Because what good is knowledge after the death that old age must be prepared for everyday? It follows from this that dictionaries will continue to exist in heaven." —*A Year of the Hunter*

I never gave it any thought
except to wonder at the argument.
When I imagine heaven,
it is the end of everything,
including speculation, quests
and questions, and looking up
words and facts,
but to those for whom the search
is all, the goal secondary, it must
be hell. Calm to them is boredom,
ennui. Their only inwardness
an inexhaustible mine, constantly
inventing new veins and tunnels,
so as never to go bust.
It's just an argument to pass the time,
lest it slip into eternity. You are dust,
like that you blew off old dictionaries,
where vandals drew obscenities,
and lovers left their names.

ELEGY FOR STUDENT DAYS

Dark library skies
full of tumbling leaves
and squalls of thought:
how can a man at sixty,
at twenty, know anymore
than what he's forgotten?
Aeschylus slipping
through a school arm,
the skate key mid-air
on its loop, hit the ground
at the same time.
Who can read this fire-writing,
scribbled on the night
with a glowing stick?
By the end, the beginning
is gone. An unheard sound
that floats in silence
forever. A ball thrown out
that goes on and on
halving the distance
between it and the wall.

THE VIEW

Climbing the stairs to my room,
at the top of the landing the light
through the dormer window makes a
familiar diamond on the floor, but
when I go over and look out, instead
of the usual view of backyards and
fences, there is a wide, calm river
flowing into the house where I stand.
On either side are grassy banks and
on the right bank two huge animals
rear up, biting and butting
their heads. And when I am afraid for
them instantaneously I am shown an
x-ray of one, how under the skin
the bone structure goes everywhere
and it couldn't be hurt, and when I
see the other's antler is torn and
soaked with blood, the thing inside
which knows says it is like a fingernail
and will grow back. Then I relax and
watch until dark as the river flows into
the house. When I awake I realize it was
a dream of the world before man.

That scene, so slow-moving and serene,
recalled in anxiety and pain, like the
shining dot you focus on to blot out
the dentist's drill, joins those other
old repeated thoughts you reach for
and hold when tired and lifeless you
seek rejuvenation in the scenes of
childhood, a long ago victory, or

memories of first love which still
move us, far as we are from them
and so hopelessly changed.

IN US LAKES ARE DRYING

In us lakes are drying,
paths are overrun with darkness,
a hand lets go another,
its pressure ending.
The warmth
evaporates,
runs to the sun
which was here
before the moon,
that, old and faceless,
now lights the way.

Right now
what are you forgetting?
The black and wet
alleyway beside the bar
we went to in the afternoon,
where everyone used to go
outside and get high;
how we matched
our hands to fallen leaves
like sizing gloves, a bridge
between two spheres,
profound and awed,
yet palm to palm,
only one alive,
still somehow you
found a pulse.

Do you ever think
as you go about your day
that inside another day is dying,

that was once 'today,'
when in the noon
of your activity and busyness
some long-ago sad hours
fraught with then-dangers
finally and harmlessly decay?

POEM

Looking at this valley
you think how a hand would
have done it differently,
evened out the hills, not left
that one irregular, jagged.
Millions of years ago the field was
a lake or channel bed
and where the tractor
is making dust, giant fins
stirred the mud. Now
the water has receded
to this trickle down the center.

Strange after approaching
slowly on the winding road
to the valley floor,
having watched the tractor's
progress back and forth
across the field, and its
long tail of dust, to find
only a boy driving.
The light in the air
seems repeated, maybe
another place you said
I'd like to live here
and meant it. Inside
they form an odd gallery
of landscapes, joined
with moments by an almost
chemical need for peace.

Put your hand in the water;
it is almost ice.
You think of Pennsylvania
and the iron ore streams.
Clear amber in the laurel.
Your arm is becoming heavy,
numb with the cold. You touch
the bottom and feel nothing.
You can't tell where your hand ends
and the stones begin.

BLACK LEAVES

How far you can see
into the woods
in early spring
before anything blooms
but after the snow
that weighed down limbs
and bushes is gone.
So much light
gets through
because only a few
tough leaves hang
from the trees
like bats,
and way back you see
a dilapidated shed
on a hill used
as a dump,
with mattresses, springs,
old windows, doors,
and off by itself
in a grove, a car's
rusting carapace,
the ruins of a forge,
a broken pump.
You're surprised
how many trees are down
or on their way, leaning
ink silhouettes against
the red protractor
of the setting sun.

Close up, on the other side
of walls and fences,
along the sidewalk,
amid plastics' weird bleaching
on wrappers and gadgets,
and fading cans
sinking in a hedge,
suddenly at your feet
a headstone
sunk in the earth,
and lying near,
like a wreath,
black leaves
underwater in a tire.

THE FEATHER

The jack-o'-lantern sits on top
like the brains of the compost heap,
aging fast, thinking deep.
The eyes cave in the sockets,
teeth sag in a senile grin,
and the liver-spotted orange skin
grows taut around the shrinking skull;
the charred bowl fills
with thoughts of snow.

Where the mower stops a few feet
of weeds and honeysuckle grows
like a wild hedge between
the tiny yard and vast cornfield
where the scarecrow wears my castoff clothes
and preaches to an inattentive flock,
collecting, as part owners
of the earth, their tithe,
after the tractors leave.

Late weeds tower in the garden
over indistinguishable rows
of vegetables rotted in their second growth
or gone to seed, and the border
of protective and decorative flowers
is blown brown and petalless by the wind
which doesn't care if it is loved or not.

At the end of a furrow
become a runway
for the slow takeoff of pheasants
I pick up a tiny curled feather;
downy and soft and pale,
with a delicate scribble
of off-white on brown.
At arm's length it's barely visible
like a match in the sunlight.

Among the husks and stubble
and in the weeds growing
out of my shadow I hunt
for a nest or another feather
but there isn't any,
this was lost alone,
in flight, or momentary rest.
I pocket it: a note
to be read later.

INSIDE WORK

Laying new pipe
for a watering trough.
Digging up the packed manure,
the locked smell leaking
from beneath each shovelful.
The posts speckled with flies,
gnawed at the bottom by generations of hogs.
The jackhammer breaks the concrete in a jagged
line
across the barn floor. In the grimy dirt
under the foundation—
half of a horseshoe buried in 1910.
Sweating, leaning on the shovel, I stare
into the barnyard at the pigs standing in the rain.

POLLOCK'S *NUMBER 1*

Before it dried, before it was,
still in cans yet to be pried open,
stirred with a stick, or brush
worn down to the nub, all handle,
moving too fast and thick
for reflection, ash fell
from above, a cigarette
in the morning getting started,
bobbing like a railroad lantern
along the tracks out west.

THE IMPOSSIBLE BOUQUET

Late at night
they appear together,
the friends of different eras
who never knew each other,
only you, but tonight
because a wall's collapsed,
from age perhaps, or simply
tiredness, they can have
a conversation, or appear
for once in the same picture,
like one of those 17th century
floral paintings the artists
worked on for months, incorporating
flowers from each season as
they blossomed, and allotting space
for those not yet in bloom,
creating in the end
an impossible bouquet.

What is it they are talking about,
so animated, yet still
under their breath, half heard
and only guessed, but from
a corner of the eye they seem
to be smiling, laughing,
each in his famous way.

WHOSE REQUIEM IS THE RAIN

Whose requiem is the rain
falling so hard it wakes
office workers in their cubicles
so they come running out
to the parking lot to put up the tops
of convertibles and roll the windows
and go back inside soaked?
The storm came unpredicted.
Now light appears like a tear
in the edge of the gray,
and the sound subsides, muffled
like drums moving off . . .

What is one life when there are so many,
a few strained faces
walking to the curb, every day
a different house, a different family
dressing for a funeral.

The papers left in the station,
or blowing in the links of a fence
are already days away,
the ink and soggy pages together
soak and sink.

Water carried indoors as darkness
on clothing, or lightness on skin,
is a memory of the memory
that begins before we become
who we briefly pretend we are.

THE RETURN

Tonight a sprinkling of stars
like voices in an empty arena,
clear and distinct;
the new moon low in the sky
like the horns
of a charging bull
the matador remembers
just before sleep.

It is not a night
as the astrologers
would say "to make new plans,"
but to draw to yourself,
as friends, the old ones,
torn, blurred with spills,
unreadable in places,
a child's scrawl
brittle with age, yet
tender to the touch of eyes
used to the new and hard.

POEM

It waits at the end
of an empty page
like the pillow of snow
on the floor
of a cage the moonlight
goes through.

Uneven dark,
part living, part dead,
so dark you reach out
and lose your hand.
It turns around
greets you
attached to a shadow
sewn to a sleeve.

What do you care
about so many
shadows,
threadbare,
wrapped around a tree,
falling over the curb?
But that one
that stood at noon
right below
the breathing, motionless
animal . . .

THE PEN AND INK TREES
AT FIVE O'CLOCK

The light falls backwards,
away from earth
and its hand-picked colors,
toward the metal hues
of heaven.
The serrated edge of rooftops
tears off a page,
reduces planes and volumes
to silhouettes,
the stage-set cut out
and painted while you
were dreaming
you could move words
without touching.

No one steps into
the aching arms of the trees tonight,
outstretched like a sleepwalker's,
or touches the trembling
filigree that holds the coral
sun in a tarnished clasp.
They stand inside a living
hush, fire-swept, charred,
the noise sucked out
like oxygen. What's left
is ash, and smoke on which
a few sparks ride.

THE SOMNAMBULIST BLUE

The somnambulist blue, narcotic sky
of early evening, when over the roofs
and wires and branches appear . . .
like something obvious suddenly remembered,
or seen, as in a picture that can be
looked at two ways, a puzzle drawing
from *The Children's Page,* whose gardens
and woods, spaces in thickets and trees,
endlessly hide faces; mouths formed
by a vine, eyes and hair made of leaves
and sky; so now, suddenly seen as always
there . . . appear, in the beginning of the night
above me, the stars, beautiful as questions:
Where is your hand? Are you asleep?

SOMETHING ABOUT THE STARS

They are blind,
but you knew that.
All those years,
there,
not seeing,
but listening
to voices,
the way a satellite
overhears a conversation
in a car
miles below.
Do you remember saying . . . ?
But it's not like that,
what you said,
but how
it lives out there,
where heat and cold
are interchangeable
with light and dark,
where metallic hisses
and whistles die
in the dark
like numbers
divided by zero,
and we become
what we are
without the skin,
without the weight
of words to hold down
what we mean,
and something in us weeps,
and something in us sings.

POEM

The letter
the night
writes to you
with the last drop
of dreams,
(unfinished sentences
disappearing
on crumbling paper)
is addressed
to a grave,
a hole in the ground
where shovels
scoop debris
from past to future,
and the present
is blown away
like the dust
you breathed
standing in a cloud
watching in the rubble
the boundary stones
of your life removed.

DUSK

When it's hard to see, children,
joggers, the other world
pushing to get in, the soul
recoils from the twist of a stem.

A silence immense as a storm
presses tonight against
the glass heat of day
which magnifies each word
until it's both heard and unheard
like a hypnotist's command:

Tomorrow you will fall backwards
into a ditch; and the numbness
at your side will reach your hand,
eyes, and neck, which together
used to stand on a green bank
and point out shadows
moving on the creekbed,
while the objects casting them
swam overhead unseen.

THE FAMOUS FUTURE

In a book
with your address
from ages ago
in the front,
the poems
you've grown old with,
torn apart,
put back together,
true as mended bones
and broken hearts,
stronger . . . weaker.
The moving page,
a patch of ink,
birds on a stream,
a vineyard on a hillside
in the snow,
gnarled roots
grasping the truth.
Your hand and the page,
foxed the same way.

IN OCTOBER

One day
out of a few
every year,
always in the fall,
everything suddenly
seems so clear,
as if there were
no air, and we
were no longer
seeing through something
but seeing things
as they are.
When even the dull
stones and sand
of the roadside
seem washed overnight,
rinsed of some
habitual stain,
the pebbles
like those from
a child's collection,
spread out on the bed,
polished with spit
to look like they did
in the stream.
Days most like
those elementary ones,
furthest from us now,
whose calendar leaves
pressed deep and long,
have gone through changes
like peat and coal

becoming diamonds,
but much quicker,
like the solution
in the beaker,
whose darkness clears
when stirred.

BEGIN HERE

Begin here. Where I began.
Across the yard, over unmarked graves
of starlings and goldfish, this house
casts the same shadow that fell
inside me twenty years ago,
darkened nerves and left them stained.
Enter where new paint on the door jamb
hides ruler marks and dates under its skin.
Climb down green stairs and ladders
to my childhood; in the rushing dark
watch secrets cross like beams of light
and shine along the bones, hunting faces
at windows in the blood.
Cross the cold calendar of memory,
the scar tissue in the mind's picturing flesh.
Touch my beginning and leave.
Rise out of coal cellars
lined with canning jars,
past rooms of upset games, into my arms
around this house the night we met.

FIRST SNOW

The earth is white today,
as if it could choose.
Torn paper fell through
the night on the school
and yard. Chalk limned
the charcoal lees of elms.
The orchard floor is
solid again with petals,
and miles of city streets
are paved with harmless stone.

Snow is beautiful because
it never changes from the day
you were a kid; the same flakes
fall in front of headlights, slant
the same way, sound the same,
when everything else has changed.
It buries years, the makes
of cars, setting the stage
for the return of earth's vanished
race of snowmen, who come back
with eyes that once were soft
and green; they stay for days
or weeks, or just the afternoon.

AT THE GRAVE OF SANTA CLAUS

A sack of bones: childhood's end,
the cord pulled tight against the spirit's
throat. Stones weep inside a tomb:
time leaves no mark on eternity,
exists only in a world that is set up to be torn
down.
What remains knows nothing of the struggle,
pain and joys of machines that dream.
Whose mistakes we are, our own
have added to, increased the soul's weight.
A toy-strewn floor in the dark
is an obstacle course to the next world.

ALL THROUGH CHILDHOOD

All through childhood were we
putting together these rooms,
these lives? Were we already
collecting the books that would
lie beside us on the nightstand,
picking out prints on the wall,
even the way the sunlight drowns
in the uncut grass outside the door?
Was that planned too? And when
the curtains are drawn shut
and the room is almost dark,
isn't that almost-darkness taken
from a time when miniature hands
covered the eyes pretending
to be closed. Though this page
in my hand didn't come from long ago
or far away this space was saved for it,
kept vacant all these years, the way
couples buy a lot and hold it
hoping to build someday.
But for what reason, to what end,
do we arrange and rearrange until
we achieve the kind of perfection
that eluded us as children, when we
controlled neither time nor space
nor the borrowed matter we placed
within them. Yet now they comfort us
like last things, tomb furnishings
we can never grow tired of,
and we're content to live again
in detail, to reclaim all the uncollected

dreams that hang like banners on the wall,
a wall we might have defaced when
we were young and drunk on the wind.

THE WALL OF LIGHT

There must be an explanation
for those tiny bursts of light
you sometimes see in the air
between a blank background
and the thing you're looking at,
suddenly just there,
the way one word leaps out
of all those sentences
to be the mirror,
or window with a view
that never changes day or night;
and when you turn
so quickly at a slightly
different angle the Invisible
explodes and sparkles
with what you called
"the pinpricks in the air"
in a poem once
to a woman who was dying.
And if I hung around with doctors,
or met one at a party
I'm sure he could explain
it just like that,
the same as the "floaters"
that used to worry you
were explained away
to nothingness, but tonight
lacking such assurances
and explanations, with all
that's gone before,
they could be for someone

longing to believe,
a clue, the proof, or chance
behind the drapery and staging
of this performance
there's a wall of light
that sometimes shows,
when the fabric's torn or wearing,
like the "wall of sound"
that used to prop up
those rock groups,
and perhaps still does,
on summer nights,
driving "the loop," circling
the deadened hearts of towns.

WHEN I CONNECT

the dots on this map
they form the figure
of a young man
running, city to city,
without direction,
lost, but always
running, until
crisscrossed with lines
his body's caught in a web
of its own making:
the face segmented
like a saint
in a stained glass window,
or one of the undecided
in the foreground,
who need to touch that robe
in order to believe.
Eventually the lines
grow thick as rope,
gone over so many times,
back and forth
as if for emphasis,
building imperceptibly
the way when children
tie you up with kite string
and colored twine,
babbling their singsong
as they orbit
giddily about you,
suddenly you find
you cannot move
and they cannot stop
or hear you.

FOR GAIL

Walking through Cambridge,
like acrobats
we step on hands
stuck to the pavement,
with raindrops deflected
from branches,
making their way down
like pinballs, glistening,
out of darkness.

Did the hands applaud?
And was it for the birds leaving,
going south, or one
of a hundred other things
we know nothing about,
like the slaughter of the worms
after the rain, on blacktop, in pools,
their bodies questioning everything?

LISTENING TO MUSIC

for.Tomas Tranströmer

Tonight, by the light
of a single star
cast on the ceiling
from the imperfect
meeting of grids
above the pilot
on the stove,
I sit at the table
listening to music,
and remember how
once I saw my soul
reduced to a dot of light
in the brain, my body
become a plastic shell
filled with a black liquid
that left me paralyzed except
to wait and watch
moment by moment
for it to engulf me,
before the drug wore off.
And then even as
the paranoia ebbed
I tried to will myself
back to that height
in spite of the pain
because it was more real.

That night I came down
from near madness
through the exhilarating
wake of fear

into a state of grace,
awed by the frailty
we live with everyday,
bolted to our sanity
and health, unaware
their shadows walk
so closely beside us.

Just as I thought
the terror would never end,
so I thought the grace
would last forever,
it felt so natural,
but it was soon gone,
imperceptibly,
as seasons change
in the city.
And although that
state has not returned,
the thought of it
is with me often.
How calm it was,
and blissful,
despite chaos
and discord, the flaws
and errors only acting
to overcome
the incompleteness
of perfection,
to break the vacuums
of abstractions,
the way tonight,

eyes closed,
the scratchy record
becomes a room
where sputtering candles
light the keyboard,
and stiff pines
scrape the windows
behind a quartet.

YOU AGAIN

1.
I knew you were dead
the minute I saw you,
or dreamed you, or you
dreamed me, however it works,
because you haven't changed at all
in thirty years. And no one
wears those clothes anymore!

You were selling *The New York Times*
on the street (though in the dream
there was no street,) like Jean
Seberg in *Breathless,* remember,
who's also strangely gone.

It has been so many years
that in the slow process of canonization
you might be a saint by now
if they overlooked youthful indiscretions,
and something called a "mortal sin."

If they were looking for
a miracle I hope they found
that night you saved a life
whose flame was guttering
in a room of used-up breaths
by throwing whiskey on it,
making it blaze again
with your incendiary talk.
And finding a place in the city
for twenty-three dollars a month.
If that wasn't a miracle

it was certainly a sign of special powers.
As for the last condition of sainthood:
after your death you've interceded
on behalf of someone who's prayed to you:
how many times the answer's come
before the question, your old trick,
and I knew you were there,
just as surely as the breath that moved
these papers on the desk wasn't mine.

2.
I don't expect to see you
in a window in a church wall, with the light
streaming around your shoulders
and your frizzy hair lit up
like a halo, arms outstretched
as if you were carrying an invisible canvas
across Astor Place on a windy day,
ready to leap down at any moment.
No walls or windows could contain
your restless energy, except
perhaps that unbuilt church,
holy place we carry in us,
which opens at the strangest hours,
when no one is near, late at night,
swaying at a party, eyes closed;
early morning kneeling in the garden,
a dozen bulbs laid out,
the ground smell overwhelming.
In a hospital elevator everyone
breathing the same air, facing
the same way, but each

in the presence of a different saint,
and all have passed
the only test that counts:
at the mention of their names
a smile comes instantly.

NINETEEN SIXTY-FIVE

You could not contain
that loneliness now,
your body would explode.

Then you went to work
with it, shouldered
planks, put up sheetrock,
hauled plaster and cement,
and at the end of the day
walked home, smoked,
drank, and read
late into the night
with the radio on.
In the dark
full of sirens and crashes,
you went to sleep
with it.

If tonight that loneliness
returned, a leaden guest,
stopping up the rivers
of your blood, would you
even know, for an instant,
before the darkness becomes
permanent, where it
came from, what ghost it was?
Or would it remain anonymous,
another of the host of unclaimed
shadows that people your
imagination, one you
might not notice passing
on the street looking

straight ahead, or would
you greet it with that warmth
and flush of recognition reserved for
those who shared your bed?

BOWERY SAVINGS

In line on Friday,
oblivious to the sky,
trees and grass,
to the sprung coils that rise
from the ubiquitous chimneys
along the wall of children's drawings,
I sign my checks, my signature
an unconscious scrawl which,
like words repeated
till they're nonsense,
begins to resemble one
of those disheveled lean–tos
now revealed
by winter's defoliants.
Sticks and vines of ink
loop and bow
and form a core
unique as the whorl
of a fingerprint:
swift, familiar gestures
distilled from hours
of strain, in a classroom
hunched over a pencil,
tightly gripped,
the tall sky outside
blank and answerless
as the paper, now
heavily erased, torn
by the light of revision.

Exchanging time and labor
like blood for cash,
we wait, drained,
paychecks in hand,

and the hands pale,
caked with plaster,
flecked with paint,
pores clogged
with grease dark as the face
at the kitchen window at midnight
that tells us more
than we want to know
about ourselves.

Pictures taped to the wall
evoke blank stares
from eyes dull,
and turned inward,
lost in counting,
the connection gone
between the mounting
paper strength of zeros
and these misshapen
beckoning stars.

Leaving the bank,
trying to walk and count,
but stumbling on the curb,
like a guy I once saw
in Tompkins Square Park,
obviously high on something,
fumbling a wad of bills,
who smiled at first
when the wind carried
some of them away,
then laughing convulsively
started peeling them off
one by one and letting them go.

NIGHT'S SILENCE

1.
Night's silence,
a space left blank
for answers. I fail
and have to read
myself to sleep,
and failing that . . . ?
The door is locked
on being awake
and alive. I think
of those who forced
the lock, how a thought
destroyed them, an image
or particular scene
that never went away
or lost its power.
And others I still share
this room with, in dawn,
or dark like this.

Scattered across time zones
in cities where we lived,
under skies the old white
of lead paint, or below
the brilliant violet midnight
in the country, are the calm
or agitated faces
of friends asleep,
at different angles
and stages, from night's
first dreams which skim
the surface of the day
for names and themes,

to other, deeper rooted ones
that end with light.

Each state fed blood
from the state before,
and sharing a light source,
dims and brightens
as we breathe,
and is accompanied by music,
though unheard, notes
struck by sleepers' hands
moving at their sides.

2.
Distance dwarfs mementos:
a scarf becomes a rag
in another city,
and the city is turned over
in a glove compartment
in a junkyard. Will I
ever see this town
as a dot on a map
and say *I lived there*?
It happened twice already.
Was it a blessing or a curse
when deep inland the plow
turned up a seashell?
Incongruous as that bottle
of Walden water saved
from a prep school pilgrimage,
that stood unopened,
undisturbed, brushed

by the hashish winds
and manic howls,
on the sill
of the phony window
between the rooms
in your apartment
on Second Avenue.
Where is it now?
Was it finally poured
into the New York City sewers,
or is it still in your bag, tossed
as you are tossed?

Between us
we probably have
more beginnings
than all the dead ends
of evolution,
the pigs with wings,
stones that spoke,
and walking flowers.
Once we saw
a starting sky
at the end of the street,
upright, gray,
a frozen stick of gum
between the buildings,
a tombstone of air
above the Hudson.

Remember Cuban bread
on the table

of the Pennsylvania farmhouse?
Outside the steamed-up windows
freezing rain,
at intervals
perhaps musical,
if heard on that scale,
instead of the hiss
of expensive gas
heating unheatable rooms,
and records repeating
endlessly as wine
fills coffee cups,
and from a corner
by the furnace,
comes, like signals
from another planet,
the sound of a typewriter
finding its first words.

3.
I am crossing years tonight
to light an answer.
What was then a handful
of cold water
dribbling back
through the fleshy cracks
of the fingers
into a pool,
is nothing now,
a cloud, many tears,
part of an ocean: memory.
And the illusory green

of the trees,
and the familiar mud
and silver of the river
at Long Level, the sky
in litmus puddles
along the road—
the taste of wine
from an uprooted vineyard.

POEM

Tired tonight
after work,
unable to stay awake
at my desk,
like the kids who
fell asleep in class
because they had night jobs
unloading trucks
or working the swing shift
in a factory.
I remember waking them
when they didn't hear
the bell at the end
of the period,
then never seeing them
after school.

Twenty years later,
my face is raised,
damp, confused,
above the fluorescent glare
of the empty page,
my forehead dented by a button,
my cheek imprinted
with the cuff's weave.
Waking now
like so many others,
unrefreshed: in a truck
pulled off the road,
or waiting outside
for the plant to open,
or in your room,

five flights up,
where you take the shirt
from the cold shoulders
of the chair,
silently lace your boots,
and buckle your belt
like a lock, slowly
putting on your clothes
as if you were putting on
a suit of lights.

SELF-PORTRAIT IN PIGSHIT

All writing is pigshit. —Antonin Artaud

I did not think—
you could not think
in that space,
crouched on those flyblown boards
laid across the tops of the pens,
nails and hammer next to you,
balancing on the beam—
about that line
I'd laughed at years before.
It was so near,
and writing so far away,
as I looked down at the pigs
no longer curious enough
to look back, thank god,
with their human eyes
from the planned pitch
of the concrete floor.

That fall, on those rainy days
we could not go
on the job,
we stayed around the farm
and worked on the *finishing house.*
The hogs already in,
we had to put up
plywood panels that
would open like windows
in summer for ventilation
and close tight in winter to form
a wall against the wind and snow.
We'd lift the panel into place

and tack it there
while we screwed the hinges
and latches on,
then pulled the nails,
but you had to be careful,
if a nail fell into the shit below
you'd have to climb down
and get it otherwise a pig
could eat it and die.

At noon, stinking, though we'd
hosed our boots
and shed our coveralls,
we were still barely welcome
at the diner down the road
where we ate every day.
It took days, even weeks
after we were done to lose
the smell. A faint
trace always lingered,
enough to take you back
to the days under the roof
beating with rain, and above
the circling, complacent hogs.

The young man smiling,
standing with his crew
in the doorway of Nellie's Café
greeted by a chorus
of catcalls and ribbing,
does not exist anymore.
Those cells are buried in the air.

Yet around his visage
there's a glow
as if someone has been breathing
on his picture, trying to bring
it closer, make it clearer.

GUARD IN A CORNFIELD

says so much:
the idea!
the picture:
at night
alone
walking the rows
listening
watching.
To what?
Shoot
the thief?

Once
I had a window
on a cornfield
and at night could hear and see
just like a cartoon
the top of one stalk go down
followed by a wrestling sound
of the groundhog
eating one ear then the other
and then across the tops
another stalk would disappear
dive under and more
devouring—
no guard
just me
back from work
standing at the window
thinking how simple
how simple

*(From a list of his work experience, made by Attila Jozsef,
in an application for relief)*

LABOR DAY

The great picnics and softball games
resist, like children fighting sleep,
the disappearance of their background,
trees and bushes blending in a darker green,
the need for jackets and sweaters,
as the ball becomes harder to see.
In the air around the empty bleachers,
ghosts run the bases, raising clouds.
The ash of cold chimneys settles everywhere;
the dust on trophies is different.

JOHNNY UNITAS

This picture is in black and white
like the TV sets in the Fifties' living rooms
where he became the name we speak
in tones reserved for those we knew.
The spiral in the autumn air
bores deep into the psyche
and physique of all who've borne
disappointment edged with pain.
Not defeat exactly, but injury enough
to leave a scar, a limp, an ache
for which there's no relief but more:
another chance to change your fate,
escape into the timelessness that hovers
over Time the way Olympus looks down
on earth, and all the mortals there
crouched before a screen on Sunday afternoon.

PIERO MANZONI

A doorway,
or huddled in one,
dark, recessed—
passers-by
glance furtively,
afraid of the hoarse request,
the threat, or temptation
off the road that leads
directly home,
away from that country
whose flag is a rag
to muffle bloody coughs,
and the dark into which
no one looks too closely,
that may go on forever
or suddenly stop short.
He died in the dark,
in the cold.
An open coffin
stood on end.
A doorway,
or huddled in one.
Who clowned,
who mocked,
who played the fool
yet left
among this century's
poignant artifacts
his "Artist's Breath,"
the balloon once tense,
full of life and ego,
now dull, deflated,

a pool of unreflecting rubber,
which recalls the question
that haunts each funeral,
where is he now
who was just here?

FOR MARY HACKETT

The most beautiful thing is a year:
its green, gold, and white wheel
turned by the wind and rain,
by the breaths of strangers
in a crowd beside you,
kept spinning by hands
lifted off of beds in unseen
benedictions of farewell.

Dry ice bubbling in the lake;
late summer, the brown water
boiling at the end of the dock.
Lost hours, watching a sunfish
defend a rock and a stalk of algae
from a school of cruising bass.
Days left empty as the pages
in an angel's diary.

And the long winds of fall,
which are the sighs
of people in the city,
cooling breaths that dry
the words scraped
on the stiff crepe of a corn husk
by a pin dipped in blood.

Then snow fine as dust
clapped from erasers
falls through the air
sparkling, coating
the ground like gesso,

with the slow
steady sound
of brushstrokes.

IN MATERA

In Matera,
where the darkness
rose from the sockets
of caves
under the city,
like a town
in Pennsylvania where
the coal fires burn
miles down,
year after year,
unquenchable,
I dreamed again
of you, so seldom
in all this time,
and not even you,
but a stranger
with news of you:
a confusing, messy tale,
a custody battle, lost jobs,
I couldn't follow it all,
and what I could conflicted
with what I knew,
but like all dreams
it had a logic
which overrules
contradictions, as when
I see my dead father now,
in whatever improbable place
and wake
believing it was real,
so through this
intermediary I felt you near,

as in another room
listening, and at one point,
in the semi–darkness,
thought it might be you,
in disguise, and wearing
glasses you haven't worn
since high school.
Still, I would have recognized
the voice, in that strange place,
enclosed like a porch
in some equatorial region,
shuttered against the heat
of the day. What were
you trying to say?
Waking, I tried
to find my way back,
there is a way,
almost by vibration,
but it was lost, and you
receded like a train
pulling out of a station,
though really it was me
who was leaving.
In the morning,
in a cold hotel,
my wife and son
next to me,
our beds in a row
like a ward,
we rose and went
down into the streets
stained with the dust

of mountains and caves,
to a church built
to the dead, whose
crowned and laureled
skulls were carved across
the door, and skeletons
danced on the lintel.
An old woman in black let us in.
Sometimes there is no message.
Just a presence,
saying "I am not lost."

SUITCASE FULL OF TEARS

Don't let the baggage handler
touch it, or the customs agent
open it, looking for contraband.
When it sloshes at your knees
your midnights knock against
you like a tide. You are the moon,
the eye that's seen it all, rolling
through the asphalt heaven,
the bone without a skeleton,
the world and world-
lessness combined.

HOMECOMING

We drove through the gates
into a maze of little roads,
with speed bumps now,
that circled a pavilion,
field house, and ran past
the playing fields and wound
their way up to the cluster
of wood and stone buildings
of the school you went to once.
The green was returning to
the trees and lawn, the lake
was still half-lidded with ice
and blind in the middle.
There was nobody around
except a few cars in front
of the administration. It must
have been spring break.
We left without ever getting out
of the car. You were quiet
that night, the next day,
the way after heavy rain
that the earth cannot absorb,
the water lies in pools
in unexpected places for days
until it disappears.

INDIAN SUMMER GARDEN PARTY

False places, air flowers, spines,
showers of spears in the ice cubes
melting on the lawn. What does the grass think?
That it's hail? That summer is over?
It is. This is a mirage.
Looking at birds, thinking they're bats,
in a staggering flight in the top
of the pines, everything outlined
in black. The last of the coffee! Rides home!
Dresses passing under the hemlock
so white and blank nothing can be written on
them.

HOURGLASS

This is the ocean floor
in two piles,
poured through a string of air.

A tide nowhere.

The way the blood moves
from the brain to the genitals
and back.

And a woman sleeping
on the beach—
all that time.

THE HITCHHIKER

I don't want to tell him
how much the place he's headed
has changed, that he won't even
be able to afford a beer there.
He looks ahead, sideways,
the sunlight mars his face,
shows he cannot
answer life's blows.
He's just an opponent now.
He digs for words. They
fall off a shovel, the stones
are names. The junk
I had to move to let him in
is still strewn across the floor
of the back seat. But his
breath on the window is gone.
I let him out near the center,
an easy walk. I know
before long, his clothes,
the crowds, youth, something,
will humiliate him.
The headlights home
will make him flinch again.

I READ THE POEM

I read the poem three times:
clever, with layered language
and meaning. When I was done
and turned off the overhead light
and settled back in my seat
a fine rain was falling, and the drops
on the bus window cast shadows
on the page as if it were wet,
or aged with a strange foxing.
Nothing I've read or imagined
could argue deeper or harder than
the two deer, one on the left,
one on the right side of the road,
or the dog, motionless on the median strip,
its black and white fur coated with dirt
and grime as if it had just come back
from running all day places it couldn't go
on a leash, rolling in stinking stuff,
then twirling three times, securing
itself to the hurtling earth,
and falling asleep.

AN OLD STORY

"How come your typewriter
is saying *thank you*
thank you thank you?"

What children hear!
Everything speaks
the language they're
trying to learn.
My typewriter which
understands nothing
says what I am trying
to understand by saying it.
Always grateful
for the chance
connection: light
through sudden darkness,
the rung missing,
the moment of weightlessness,
when the heart
without gravity
falls toward illumination.
The brake: remembering.
The filter: years
of learning
which things speak,
which sounds are important,
which can be ignored,
until we hear only a fraction
of what's around us,
feel just a portion
of our emotions
screened from their source.

How the world outside
seems to move
to the music indoors,
huge swaying trees
as dancers "speak"
with their limbs,
the grass parts
for an invisible guest,
and the whole scene
trembles and waves
and continues waving
after the record ends
in a kind of sign language
no one understands.
My son stands quietly
at the window
watching the world
dissolve in breath,
and listening
to an old story
whose words
are worn away.

TREASURE ISLAND

for my son

Beside me
on the couch,
finally quiet
after running all day;
his knees stick out
like a pair of bruised peaches.

The room is bright,
a box of light
floating in darkness.
Windows on three sides open
so it's almost out-of-doors.
The noise of the swamp
drifts in: peepers,
and unknown wings
flapping, shaking loose,
bugs bouncing off screens,
the corners murmuring.

Although he can read now,
he'd rather listen,
like getting a ride
and watching the trudging
miles go by.
What does he see
as I read the description
of the bluff above the cove
where the pirate ship
lay anchored?
A hill nearby
where Truro

curves around the bay?
And he's Jack Hawkins I'm sure,
but who's the Squire, the Doctor,
and Long John Silver?

Citronella circulates
its smell from childhood,
now mimicking hashish,
and the lighthouse
from a mile off
casts its weak strobe
over land, together conjuring
another treasure hunt,
begun before you've got
an idea what you're
looking for, only
what it is not.
Behind the laced sugar water
taste the metal of the spoon,
like blood, and hear again
the heroic music turning tinny,
as everything slows
like a film caught until
it burns in front of
the projector's naked bulb,
a light behind the eyes
that won't go out.

That time is kept alive
like a match cupped
against the wind, a candle
in a skull, flickering tonight

in uneven breaths,
as sleep,
the dark sub-text,
the undertow
in the story-teller's voice
pulls him under, and carries
him off to an island
overgrown with the vegetation
of dreams and peopled
by composites
from the day's dismemberment
by clock hands.

Then, subtly altered, its mass
magnetized, his head
is charged with dreams,
and leaning next to mine
generates their waking
counterpart: wishes,
but all in the negative:
may he avoid this,
be spared that,
not have to go through
something else . . . the list
cuts out a silhouette, faceless,
blind with bliss,
while I revisit another night,
an afternoon stretched into evening
in a dealer's pad on Eleventh Street,
across the table from Bobby Driscoll,
who, someone told me later,
"played the kid in *Treasure Island*."

Even the small town paper
I was reading a few years later
carried the wire service obituary,
an overdose:
a clear proof of something
still unclear.
That night
when his connection came
he broke off talking
and tied his ascot
around his arm
and hunted for a vein,
then leaned back, eyes filled
with appreciation, overwhelmed
as soundless applause
spanned the living pain
separating the same person
years apart.

The dark is lined with fur,
fins, and feathers
rustling and fluttering,
their sudden silence
a trip wire across the lawn
leading to the swamp
where the tireless lighthouse
flashes its ambiguous message:
equal parts safety and danger,
and its strobe shows
the night at work:
its jumping eyes, and vines
of climbable shadows,

and interlocking circles
like magician's rings
spreading across the water
as rain brings music,
changing tempos, slowing, adding
a thousand strings
in all directions: so many
leaves struck, grasses bent,
and branches glazed.
He stirs at its cold scent;
a shiver runs through him,
then me. It's late.
I mark our place.

LETTER TO Y

The fields are shadows,
the leaves not yet fallen
no more than words.
Difficulty everywhere,
states of being: ice or snow,
sleet or rain, tears pulled back
in a sigh. We are leaving cause
and reason here like reflections
the dark has come upon,
or wind has moved its hand over
and made disappear . . .
Your face appears in the running
stream, a frontispiece,
submerged, still boyish, though
red dye tints the page.
Out of a silver age you came,
night when the snow was
falling blindly. Looking for . . .
a toy behind the house,
a sled left where one moment ends
before the next begins?
Your voice gave out where
the dirt path met the paved road.

LOUISE

Met again in a dream—
not so long—fifteen,
twenty years.
I have gone forward.
The world doesn't see.
The voice I hear
is older
but the same.
Friend in the head,
old friend,
approaching winter,
the trees are thicker,
but bare.
The days unroll
like grade school posters
with handprinted signs pinned on:
places, names—
yours is one.

THE COLD I CAUGHT
AT THE FUNERAL

So much kissing.
Remembered closeness.
The aching later
as if I'd dug the grave
myself and laid him in it.
Tears that sprang
from nothing ran together
as one river down
our cheeks.
Around my skin and bones
another layer's added,
tightened, glowing
like that skeleton outfit
I wore at Halloween,
when we were friends.
Now I bear a different aura,
the kind that fever brings,
that deposits inside the tree
a darker, thicker ring,
as if to prove all years
are not the same, how some
with heavy winters come,
or droughts, or fire, yet end.
Though *it,* I suppose,
is still alive, the cold,
the germ, making its way,
from room to room
around the world,
through a kiss or word;
city by city,
across countries, from first

to last on the ship's manifest,
then setting forth
on a new continent,
while we are stranded here,
you in the ground, so cold
and hard it hurts to walk,
the wind about the ankles,
whispering, of this and that,
what's to come.

I AM GLAD

I am glad I saved
none of your letters.
They follow me now
only as abstractions:
flags of a country
that no longer exists.
Not a word or phrase,
survives to wound me
the way a broken trail
into another life
invariably does,
its silence glancing back
and forth as if two
worlds could be compared
when only one exists.
The other inhabits
a realm of physics,
speculation on paper,
to be presented
at a conference:
the incalculable distance
and the temporary unity
of opposites, so dry
and devoid of color,
yet no one listening
gets up to go.

Those papers, shuffled
endlessly, and ill-read,
filled with worlds
realizable only under conditions
of extreme temperature,

intense pressure,
and the suspension of time—
those are the letters I gave up,
believing one world was enough.

A NIGHT LIKE THIS

On a night like this
you can imagine
the end of the world:
the power out,
high winds and snow,
the earth changed so completely
in a matter of hours.
Total silence of manmade things,
the plows and sanders useless.
The weight of the sky
now equal to that of the land.
And the flame of the candle
you carry so frail it sways
in each breath, and with each step,
a butterfly at rest, moving its wings,
the last thought of those you'll miss,
alive in your hand.

CERVETERI

Preternaturally pristine,
preserved intact,
toys from a child's tomb,
behind the glass
in the archeological museum
where a small hand
holds you back
to see closeup
wheels that never turned,
a bell that never rang,
clay with ears and horns
and wings unchipped
by hours of play.
The past as real
as suffering
in a dream,
where there are no tears,
only sweat,
that leaves the sheets
wet as rags doused
with kerosene,
yet unlit.

BREAD AND RAIN

In the rain
a woodpecker
bangs his beak
against the trunk
of an apple tree
about to bloom.
At eye level
through the slider,
he's doing what he's
supposed to do.
When the sky clears
suddenly it's summer,
but underneath
where the roots grow
to the other side of the world,
rebels in Eretria
are moving again
through parched and blowing land.
A commander thumbs
the pages of a tract
with sand-smoothed fingers,
for words that can adapt
to any season, situation,
drought or famine,
and sprout a vision
that will survive
like the mirage
which thrives on emptiness.
And far below us in Peru,
another army is moving swiftly,
like our gleaming athletes,
carrying runners' weights,

punishing themselves,
climbing the mountain
at Tempe, taking extra laps
around the pool, training
for a meet: while these
pack nothing inessential,
and go without self-exhortation
and neon clothing, through
the green jungle at night
in single file, a snake
whose segments are
different ages,
have already gone
through many skins
and perhaps
no one piece
will see both
the beginning
and the end.

A starling chases a smaller bird
from the porch railing
where sodden bread crumbs
cling like early fallen blossoms,
though here there is more than enough.
Bread, and rain.

LETTER TO AN ANCESTOR

Leaf-eater, planter,
man of pure water,
there is no water here
that is pure,
that is not host
to rotting chemicals and disease,
that does not make
a dark poisonous crease
through the cities,
that is not lined
with the walls of mills
and factories,
that does not flow
slowly under bridges
full of suicides.
The snow is darker every year,
and the moon wears chains
to a corner of this house.

LANDSCAPE

Beautiful words
that are compressed valleys,
miles of river
and long chains of hills
in a few breaths and syllables,
these names
in tandem rattled off
on the late news;
old Indian names
beside generic ones,
Aliquippa and Oil City,
Nanticoke and Minersville,
the yearly litany
of playoff teams,
their buses already returning
through blighted downtowns
to snowy stations
thronged with fans,
while somewhere else tonight,
where the profits flowed,
in that proverbial
house upon the hill,
the evening ends,
and a strand of pearls,
like bubbles from a flooded mine,
is returned to its case.

BLACK MAN FISHING
IN THE POTOMAC BASIN

Still as a bronze,
with a lowered sword,
he waits to set the hook
in a carp as it runs
with the bait between its lips,
then stops to swallow
in the grainy dark.
The carp's broad turn
the flash of gold coins
and broken glass
below the lacquered bridges
of palatial lawns where
paisley gowns reflect
as oil slicks,
or in the concrete embankment
of this polluted basin
where the froth of cherry blossoms
sloshes in a mass against
the shore like gutter snow,
and in the mirrored sky
a rainbow spans
the buckling monuments.

REVOLUTION IN THE AIR

Reading how this party split
into two factions, one of which
survived into the '90's, the other
dissolved almost immediately
over disagreements as to whether
to concentrate on cadre-building
or developing alliances within
the working-class . . .
I had to keep one finger
in the back, in the glossary,
to keep track of who's who,
and remind myself these acronyms
had faces, marched on sunny days,
in rain and wind, argued
endlessly the course of events
that never came but flowed away
from them on a tide of breaths
propelled by heartbeats, little oars
that move us closer, through
narrowing passageways,
to the future's source.

FEBRUARY

The murder of Malcolm X
took place long ago
but now he's everywhere,
coming up from underground
the first thing you see,
books with his face on the cover
on a cloth spread out
on the sidewalk next to T-shirts
on which a splotch of colored ink
mixes with nothingness
to form his eyes, the edge
of the familiar jaw and brow.
He was in transition then,
the crowds that themselves
were thinking, rethinking,
knew it was important, even brave,
to come, the nadir of the winter,
dark hole of the week, Sunday
afternoon, the street all dirt
and wind, corrupted snow.
That is also when Horowitz
always played, Sunday
afternoon, at 4 P.M. . . .

He was dead by then,
on stage, among cables
and wires from microphones
and tape recorders,
freed from his age
in its swollen strings,
untuned, like a bead

curtain you push aside
to enter a room
denied to others.

THE BUDDHAS

The earth's too photographed,
too little seen,
its life sucked out
to preserve a shell.
You're among invited ghosts,
to tour the debris:
the hulls of used-to-be
and would-be worlds.

1.
The photos show
the world a rockface,
plain but for two
gigantic statues
carved into the wall,
and at the base,
almost unnoticed
because they're small,
insignificant black holes
like punchmarks,
that are the openings of caves
that honeycomb the cliff.

It's possible to climb
the whole way now,
through narrow passages
and painted chambers,
the quarters where
monks and pilgrims
lived, and come out
high above the valley floor
inside the windy niche

where the Buddhas
stood and looked across
to mountains far away.

But the great stone heads,
like great stone heads
everywhere, saw nothing
that was before them,
neither the flashing waves
on the shores of Easter Island,
nor the jungle vines
that drape themselves
like peekaboo fingers
about the eyes
of Mayan gods; their
gaze is inward, toward
the meaning of the eye,
how sight takes place,
electrically, not moving
along a wire, but being
changed, the way
thoughts change, are there
without the cause
that brought them,
but leave in a chain
that follows laws we made.

2.
How could the world
love these aggregates
of grains blown off
harder rocks

then recombined
to form this coarser stone
more than the multitude
of faces, torsos, and hearts
visibly beating between
their glaring ribs, waiting
for help that never comes?

Once again the ageless
question surfaces,
that appeared in
Decembrist days:
"Shakespeare for a pair
of shoes?" then was lost
for decades, buried
under layers of forgetfulness
that blew across distracted
years. The time it takes
to dig them out
is the time it takes
to live and die.
Meanwhile new barriers
have been thrown up
against our knowing
how our lives oppress
unseen figures fighting
for air among our
exhaled breaths.

3.
Two blindnesses, neither
pure, each admitting
light, coarse and fleeting,
drag themselves across
the desert of the page:
like fronts of hot and cold air
meeting, whose collision
lights what isn't there.

TAKE A NUMBER

These stories, parables
and anecdotes
are juxtapositions
of the new world,
the 21st Century arriving!
How a junkie's jive
enters a stately hall,
marches up the table
at Thanksgiving
like a parade of ants
is ordinary now,
yet new because we haven't
gotten used to it, and by the time
we do, the room will be painted
another color, even wallpapered
like it used to be,
before us, and speaking
in our places, parking where
we're parked tonight,
will be new people, people
with long, funny (to us) names,
who specialize in things we've
never heard of, and if you're lucky,
a child will come running into the room
with your curling picture and say
"Who's this, I found it behind
the refrigerator?"

IN THE MUSEUM
OF NATURAL HISTORY

Walking among the bones of animals that will
never return.
One of them. Useless today
against the tide of gleaming slickers carrying the
yellow
from the daffodils across the street,
gathering around a central figure counting heads.
A spreading puddle of rainwater at their feet.

Out of earshot,
my quiet, their noise,
both superficial
compared to the primordial silence
of bones, and the deep cries
from the room of Oceanic masks
whose open mouths gasp
for air in a climate-controlled environment.

Uneasy at windows in museums,
standing in the stairwell
or a hall between exhibits
after looking hard all afternoon,
I'm suddenly self-conscious
as before a mirror, but anonymous
as the wet roofs, steam from ducts
and vents, the scene of the truck
maneuvering in the yard below:
the view which represents the flesh,
while what's inside, which never moves,
behind the eyes that looked out
of skulls and masks,
needs no name, may be extinct,
yet aches today all the same.

NOTEBOOK

Jade darkness
beneath the arches
of a mountain road.

Haze of wood smoke
over the valleys
in the burning season.

The tires kick up leaves
in a village square,
and in courtyards and gardens
and behind walls
dingy with the perpetual stain
of cars and trucks
the candelabrum and menorah
of the pollarded plane trees
stand unlit in the Sabbath dusk . . .

Where we visit, what we see
and remember and write down,
carries light from that place
to the next, until at last,
at home, on a cluttered nightstand,
the festive edge of a page
torn from a spiral notebook
flutters in the sleeper's breath,
and confetti blows through a dream.

IN ANOTHER LIFE

But there is no other life.
Nowhere can we change
what's wrong in this one
as they do in tryouts
of a play, or in
an interactive story
that can still end differently:
she might come back,
the clouds part and shower
gold and light on a heart
caged in a box
weighted down with stones,
that once held pleasures,
the kind you bury
with a plan to return,
but the road changes,
narrows, and you forget,
remember only
in a lonely room in a city
too far away.
Then you change
and it no longer matters.

But to that place—
where nothing's yours,
and everyone's a stranger,
two minutes in any direction
and you're lost,
where the coat you're wearing
against the wind
(now soft and fresh like Spring

still months away)
will be your last—
there are buses every day.

POEM

I felt nothing
driving by your city,
no magnet tug
greater than any other,
just old water tanks,
oil reserves, malls
and miles of fast-food restaurants
and struggling store fronts
pulling for a different
reason; none of it
has any hold on me,
but looking down
those long streets
of little houses,
with trees grown up,
the driveways overflowing,
and the shining acres of cars
bowing down before
a single god, I didn't
hear one heartbeat
above the motor,
or words like music
caught in the hollows
of a swing set,
or any other place
the air stagnates:
a box with grass
and water, stars
punched in the top
so we can breathe.

HITCHHIKING

Waist-high weeds
and leaning sticks
with different colored ribbons,
machines in a pasture,
necks stretched to earth.
This is the beginning
of a school or hospital,
the sign with its back to me
says which, by whom,
for how much,
but coming from
an access road,
looking for the town,
and walking through a field
turning into a block
in a future development,
with the hydrants and drives
already in, just waiting
for buildings,
and the grasshoppers
flying in the dusk
under a lineless sky,
for me it is a place
to rest and think,
holding to
a changing destination.

WINTER DAWN

From snowbank to snowbank
like beds, yanked
and let go
by invisible hands,
I stumble home
at closing time,
tacking the asphalt
in a wind of glass,
the pantomime
of a man pursued
by ghosts.

Around the bend
on Shankpainter Road,
all groundlight gone,
more stars wear through,
the universe is close,
personal,
the hurtling Milky Way
a wisp of snow
across the drive,
the dead streetlamps
like thoughts not worth
putting into words,
the wind of slamming doors.

Glasses on,
I wake to a test pattern,
further downstream,
carried by the dreamless
river of alcohol,
to surface by the city

of the bedside table,
where the foliage
of crumpled bills
surrounds a lake
of coins which sprawls
before the skyline
of bottles, cans, and vials.

And then to drift,
into a second sleep,
where broken glass
sifts slowly down
through cloudy depths,
and sparkles in the beams
of flashlights as they
probe and pan where
someone threw the keys.

ALBA

for Abby and Bob

Waking in the wrong room
at the wrong time: dawn,
its fool's gold makes
everything beautiful,
any hand tender; waking in it
you don't wake up
but surface somewhere above waking,
still dreaming. The town from a cloud.
An aerial view of the fishing village,
the rows of white dollhouses, the toy boats
floating on the harbor, the streets
deserted, the only ones up
a policeman standing in a doorway
and a man with one shoe
retracing his steps.

TOY SOLDIERS

The paint is chipped from their uniforms from many battles and the quickly arranged Armageddons before supper. Lead stares from the broken ends of spears and swords, always the first to go, later, the irregular openings where arms were, or hands that held flags and reins. In each of them is a portable void, unencumbered by organs or consciousness. Lame horses are propped against the leg of the sofa.

The flesh of the hands extends over the cuffs, chins are cut off by high collars. Dabs of red and gold, for buttons and epaulets, miss their raised targets. One eye is lower than another; the mouth is off center.

Still, they march through the world, peering over newsprint shields in the library, lowering their visors along the bar.

LITTLE ELEGY

Even the stars wear out.
Their great engines fail.
The unapproachable roar
and heat subside
as wind blows across
the hole in the sky
with a noise like a boy
playing on an empty bottle.
It is an owl, or a train.
You hear it underground.
Where the worms live
that can be cut in half
and start over
again and again.
Their heart must be
in two places at once, like mine.

MEDITATION IN THE PARK

Magnified by tears,
little lives seem insignificant
until we see they're just like us,
prisoners of the dust,
vacillating
between abstraction,
the shadow of the real,
and the heaviness of flesh,
always being here,
in the present with no escape
that follows them and us
like a sun that to someone
far-off and thinking
only of the beautiful
must appear as a star
to wish upon.

We are surrounded by others
who share our fate,
the park alive
with struggle, war
in the grass between
the four and six-legged creatures,
their triumph or disaster,
the birds' inevitable homing
to gravity's call,
darker than sleep.

The always nervous
squirrels and pigeons,
and slaughter everywhere,
worms embedded in the lens,

the daily falling of the leaves,
a smear across the road,
that stain all but gone—
but underneath, in the careful
burrows, and nests
or less, crevices and cracks,
life holds on:
the microbe's automatic spirit,
all the way back to strands
that bear life's codes, impossible
to disobey, even after
fear skews a surface
already troubled by our breathing
as we peruse up close
orders to be free.

There are galaxies within arm's reach,
their infinitude unseen
but felt, stars
behind the stars,
worlds inside the clods
the programmed insects move,
their lives complete
systems without question,
but alive nonetheless.

RAIN

It is the sea coming back to us,
and the lakes and streams you never saw
the bottoms of, it is the fountains in front
of great houses and public buildings
and in the middle of those busy traffic islands.
It brings no news from those places;
all their taste and odor has been worn off;
it comes down pure, distilled, nameless.
Yet under streetlights where it turns shadows
into reflections, attaching features to silhouettes,
you find a face in the trembling mosaic:
parts of it, the lips, the cheeks, the nose,
are yours, but the eyes are the sea's.

WORKING IN WINTER

We could fall.
The branches are slippery enough.
January in the top of a maple.
A tree-saw hanging from my belt.
Who are you?
What are you doing up there?
The sidewalk blows away.
It feels good. The air is crazy,
filling with snow. Cars maneuver
around the piles of branches
in the street. The cuts
smelling of fresh wood.
The snow and sawdust
falling together.

POEM

Across gravel that has lost
the secret of the mountain,
dust which hides in an insect's voice,
through what's left of the tattered shade
that stunted love
so it could stay in a world
guarded by toy soldiers,
a boy leads you to your shadow.

WORKING ALONE

There is no one
for miles,
for years,
and the snow
that's piled up
along the highway,
that you must write on,
melts each spring,
is washed away
by tears
you imagine
someone else
is crying.

In a used-up corner,
where the shadows
are folded shut;
against the plaster
you feel shivers
of the wind,
the rumbling of stones
turning over in their sleep
on the river bottom.

Mark this wall,
the strangeness
that has lost its luster
to the smoke and ash
of dredged-up words:
knowledge wasting form
in explanation.

Cobwebs connect
things from a beach:
the feather, the shell,
pebbles, glass,
and wood worn
smooth as skin,
along the sill.

The room bursts into flames
when you leave,
your old breaths still burn,
ignite the dust of autumn/
spring, hinges
that bear the weight
of turning
green and gold
in the world before
next: earth without us.

SECRET OF THE ALPHABET

Secret of the alphabet,
egg of zero
cracked and giving birth
to endless numbers,
show me
the snow's annihilation in the rain,
the attrition of deltas,
the extension of ladders
into weary air at sunset
where breath follows breath
in a long broken chain
like the wavering flight of bees:
the perforation where you tear
earth from its flamboyant shadow.

Look at the rain;
it makes everything
less important.
The years ahead
hardly lift their eyes
to see what invisible ink
has written on our breath.
We claim a link
with everyone who ever
stopped and left a thought,
used the rain along the way
the way a bird uses a string,
weaves it into its return.

Who are your priests?
The rakers of leaves,

hairdressers of the dead,
forgotten neon soldiers,
makers of the last coffin?

Restrain the waves
in this room
launched from the background
of a photograph.
Quiet the ghost
singing to himself
beside the radio.
The window develops morning
like a shadow under the bridge
of last night's talk.

SOME NIGHTS,

between the car and door
in the dark
I look up to find
the great river
of the Milky Way,
and stand for minutes
growing cold
in the autumn air,
unable to move,
take my eyes away,
only to look back,
wishing the house
would vanish,
and I was alone,
far from lights and roads,
with *its* dark, *its* cold,
its change
from everything known,
which makes even
those reaching claw-like
backyard trees
seem welcoming,
and I think this must be
how innocents are drawn
into madness,
a whispering begins,
that could be anything, the wind,
but then turns definite,
becomes a voice that has
but one intended listener.

In a field years ago
I watched another river, dark,
without a name or end, flow overhead,
hundreds of thousands of birds,
the complete opposite, the negative
of that silent, lifeless stream of stars.

The cornfield is gone, so are the birds,
though their descendants may
still follow that same flyway,
perhaps some stars are also dead,
and only their light survives
like a memory a million years old.

Tired and cold, under
icy reminders of how insignificant,
how brief we are, I mouth
their message in words I see
disintegrate: I am alone;
I am almost nothing.
Yet these rivers meet in me.

SHADOW PLAY

To complete the thought . . .
the day grows dark,
and at the top,
where the candlesticks and stairs,
the clouds and stars
should be,
an image
blocks the light
like a wing,
a door dangling
from one hinge,
a realization
the way you came
does not go back.
And those figures
in the street,
leaving
one by one,
were guides,
without words
or explanation,
lamps,
now going blind,
and around their hollow bases
shadows run
like sheets of rain.

ALCHEMY

Piles of leaves burned in the gutter
and smoke rose like the trunks
of phantom trees and hung
over the street, sifting ash
onto the curb as residue
of the alchemy that turned
extraordinary gold into something rarer:
its fragrance.
And when the sun died
the moon came up
and rolled like a battered hubcap
across the sky.

Who looks back
through glasses now too weak
and scratchy from the drawer,
goes down a list
of crossed-out names—
moved, and *moved* again,
until they disappeared.

The sky yawns
and swallows years,
the way a field
becomes a suburb,

and the last thing you saw
in that stinking creek
was something caught
far down, pale, blurred
through the too thick lens
of the current, gone
when you looked again.

FOUR POEMS

1.
Tonight
with the moon's thin dime
I'll call the dead.
They're ready
with their answers:
Live! Explore!
who did nothing of the kind
in life but are empowered
now to implore others
with cheap advice.
To have the answer
is not the answer:
every student knows
it's worse than useless
to put down a number
read off someone else's paper
if you can't show how you got it.
And it's not what they know
but what they don't
that interests me:
things still here
that hold them,
of which they can't let go,
as if, after a tornado
that took first their homes,
then their clothes,
then their bones,
in what is left
(which is invisible to us)
they sift and hunt,
ask odd questions,
that make me think

of others
also dead,
times and places,
on my own
I'd never revisit.
Is the paper still published?
How many points does
the maple leaf have?

2.

What are you covering up
with newspapers?
What do those wings hide,
one at a time,
soaring over the kitchen table,
a magic carpet,
flung on linoleum
it's hard to believe
someone once chose,
and those magazines
with their patterns
of gloss and matte
interlocking, making faces,
continents, and coastlines,
that vanish if you think.
From afar the sound
of knocking on a door,
or walking on a grave,
equally hollow.
And only part of you
(is the sad secret)

understands.
The other part
that is in shadow always
(because if you are talking
you cannot listen),
with that moon you call the brain,
and heart you call the sun,
cold and hot in their galaxies,
which in any other universe
would cancel each other out
becoming one, but here
must endure separately,
each staring enviously
into the other's blindspot.

3.
You forget blue,
the ocean, the color
of your eyes,
and of the playground
wall already peeling,
flakes like falling sky
from a painting of
the first afternoon
you notice winter's gone,
curling off in long strips
like waves beneath
a wooden hull,
and under those disappearing
skies and seas, the brick wall
exposed like flesh
whose color you will also

soon forget.
The red within
that does our breathing,
reasoning, holds up
the heavy jar of names
and things, keeps it
from tipping over,
dribbling secrets
whose insignificance
will grow with each step
back through Eden
and the namelessness
beyond.

4.
So many visions
run out of steam—
the first three verses
of a new Revelation—
then the angel stops
dictating, content
with what it's said,
and the words are stranded,
alone with their power
and beauty attached
to nothing,
left in the hands of a toy:
a mechanical man,
a locomotive going round in circles:
all day the logger delivering
and reloading the same stack
of perfect logs, until one falls

out of the hooks,
a cup's knocked over
in surprise, the water
causes a short, the house
burns down, everyone dies.
This is why,
in the mountains,
by weak light,
kerosene, candles,
the flickering end
of a frayed extension
cord, black set type
turns to snakes
in one man's eyes;
another sees the dancing
that goes to Hell,
the music still in his head
as he steps outside—
mist like sea smoke
rising from the hills
of great stone waves
that lift the house and porch
on their voyage toward dawn,
all the booze and cigarettes gone,
the stars turning their backs,
a fire coming on.

THERE

I am far ahead
when I close my eyes,
already there,
where the dead ends
of the future lie
like lines down
after a storm,
and the avalanche of words
ends in an ellipsis
followed by dead air.

Fear is behind me,
down a long aisle
of lost breaths.
Needs that were sharp,
insistent,
are barely audible
above the building quiet.

The rest
is unimaginable:
how the voice
in the head
grows silent,
the lights
of the body
dim,
and nothing
happens next.

LULLABY

The painful series
of operations that
culminate in death:
becoming forty, eighty,
neither one. Dying young
or old, awake or drugged,
or pleasantly unaware
in sleep as they say Auden
wanted to and did, with just
the slightest sensation,
like a sleeping baby
handed from one pair of arms
into another.

AS IF

It's as if this were the last day
and these the last people
you would see,
grown close and quiet,
like a silent film,
where the faces fill the screen
with intelligence and emotion
stronger because it is in
black and white.
Here are souls—
in the elevator,
at the window—
"the light greater from within,"
like deep-sea fishes
whose bones glow and whose
flesh is transparent.

As if this peach
were the world's last . . .
and all the orchards
that Mandlestam called
"the dancing classes of trees,"
were gone, and with them
those hills, backroads,
and woods, your childhood
now a paper out of date,
an expired license, the receipt
for a meal long ago only you
can remember, taste
not just food but
talk and light.

As if these words were
the last you will hear,
not part of words' endlessness
like chains of colored paper
strung around the room
until, about to run out,
someone always finds
another strand
and keeps it going,
but the very last
before the head goes blank,
its thoughts now loud
and incomprehensible,
colors without names,
shapes meaning nothing
suggesting nothing,
but like lightning through
the rain–clotted screen,
still beautiful,
whatever it means.

THE DOORWAY,

seen a thousand times,
then changed suddenly,
the same steps followed
again and again
in the alchemist's experiment,
the same ingredients each time
except the time and its spirit,
leads to this room
where we stand by accident
and for a moment the dark lock
we live in is lighted
and we breathe the key.

VÉZELAY

From the roof above,
leaves and the detritus
of leaves are swept away
like the fog by fresh winds
that rake the slates
and swirl in the crevices
behind the saints,
whistling down the eaves,
and growling softly
in the throats of the gargoyles,
lifting the dust and dirt
of pigeons, loosed from
the gutters by the rain.

The air in the nave
has stood still all night,
a transparent column,
immobile as stone,
and undisturbed until
this morning when
a small door opened
within the large door
like the entrance
of a dollhouse, fluttering
the solid hologram of air
in which we move.
Dwarfed by the giant transept,
we step around the set-up chairs,
down to the crypt
where in a grated niche
the reliquary holds

the cloth and bones,
now labeled dubious
by Rome.

Though the fog
has been rolled away
and the sun has risen
over the trees,
inside the cold remains,
as the *Om* of bells
magnified by stone
travels through us
like the disintegrating
bones of martyrs
held above the crowd.
In this vastness
that we take personally,
as a presence,
or an absence,
in this damp and gloom,
we see our breaths,
because in here
we are either more,
or, like ghosts,
less alive.

CHARTRES

Hidden by folding chairs arranged
for the installation of a few new priests,
there's a labyrinth in the floor,
that leads as many journeys do,
to a place hardly different from
where you started, though
light-years away in another sense;
designed so that after following
its deliberate meandering and attempts
to awaken your soul, you end up
standing under the same roof,
on the same ground, in the same
light streaming in, outside yourself.

POEM

Recklessness is beauty,
Ashbery says. When a car
door opens in the dark
at ninety miles an hour
what rushes in is beauty.
The wind's hymns are
inaudible, the words
chased off by scarecrows
from the blurry fields.
The murmuring heart
beatless all those moments
waiting to see if you
will live. A hundred
thoughts of a flock
dispersing,
or just one.

IN THE CITY

Night silvers the windows.
In the glass behind the gratings
we become the thieves we fear,
then recognize ourselves:
merely prisoners
of that fear.

Down in the street
breaths like souls ascend
from bodies trapped
between the steamy underground
and frozen heaven
where the stars
form like crystals
too cold to snow.

We lived in the mind,
the city in the body,
where Mondrian's trees,
struck by lightning,
flew apart, each
branch became a street,
each patch of leaf
and sky a block
any color but green.

Retired visionaries,
still too serious,
suffering in a movie.
The ice gives way behind us,
stepping over the gutter snow,
a see-through moon slides down

below the cardboard outline
of tenements: a set
too painful to acknowledge,
too profitable to strike.

The aperture closes
in the morning light,
and the focus narrows.
Older, we know more
and see more, but
the zone of feeling dwindles;
we know what we should feel
as the gap time opens
between emotion and idea
widens too far
for any spark to leap.

TOO YOUNG TO SLEEP

Too young to sleep.
Night's glittering train
pulled through the streets
like a magic carpet on which
to ride above the tarred rooftops
and moonlit vacant lots
sparkling with broken glass.

We are searching for
a lens, a way of seeing
what we feel, the way
the telescope and microscope
reveal dark or transparent space
to be something else, a hole,
the center, a place you walk to
in a storm, the ache drugs try
to reach, a glowing stone
you hand at death to someone else,
the you you missed, could not
connect, except odd times
you felt divine, guided by
a rightness, a mantle that
fell on you, weighing nothing
and invisible, yet may have
been there all along.

Night gone,
its sparkles
fall from your hands like sand
getting up from the beach,
escaping a tide.
Thoughts retreat,

go back in the mind,
old and dark,
like the deepest part
of the river,
and what lives there
lives forever.

AT THE ART STUDENTS
LEAGUE, 1965

1.
The evening classes over,
the students and instructors,
models and monitors, gone;
the building finally empty,
the staircase clear
which was crowded all day,
and in the studios the plaster
busts and crockery,
the cloths that drape
the pedestals wait to be
arranged a billionth time,
unexceptional except
they appear in drawings
and paintings on walls, in closets,
from here to Sacramento.
And around the room easels,
carefully placed like models,
hold their pose all night,
waiting to be changed.

In the cafeteria
on the floor below,
legs up, the chairs
like cartoon dead,
stacked on tables;
no din of trays or silver
disturbs the stillness.
Every table is empty, available,
where generations
fought their battles,

and salt and pepper shakers,
and catsup bottles, and
napkins just so, illustrated
points lost upstairs in paint.

Finally dark but for
the regulation lights above
the stairwell and exits,
and outside the "smoker,"
where we held critiques
and I first learned
the amazing range
of self-justification
and of the need to please:
I want the colors to be muddy.
Or *Do you think I should
take the faces out?*
*Would it be better
greener, grayer, redder?*
Acquiescing to the slightest doubt,
or most contradictory suggestions.
Our teacher told the story,
not apocryphal, but
coming true each day,
of a painter in the forties,
who made black, instead
of white, the basis of his palette,
adding a little to each color,
to unite and pull together
the disparate elements:
the black now showing through,
his paintings darken yearly.

I pictured them like
portraits in ancestral homes,
or hung too near a chimney:
flesh turning gray, sockets
deepening as eyes recede
beneath layers of soot
and smoke. Only these
paintings, which parody
inherent vice, darken
from within, and no amount
of cleaning will bring them back.

Now the darkest building
on the block, a hole
that sucks in light . . .
names and faces first,
the voices last . . .

2.
I no longer paint
but look at paintings
as if they were
extensions of that self,
relics of an unlived life.

Of the others I suppose
only the dullest were
unswayed by the continuous
music of the street, or
words from platforms that bent
each mind and heart
in new trajectories.

Whoever was not drawn
into that maelstrom,
where action vied
with contemplation,
sacrifice with self-indulgence,
has nothing now to say;
who never grasped
"the something more":
that art is just a hook
to draw us back
to a place
we've been
before there was art
but now cannot reach
without it.

TRIPTYCH

1. Nothing's Changed

A life you led
wants you back,
beckons
from the doorway
of a room where
the hours dissolve
beneath a broken clock.

And sitting there
are the brothers
and sisters of the people
you used to drink with,
their faces mottled and pale
from years of being
carried in a wallet,
pulled out only for proof
of some connection
to the world.
Now you've forgotten
their language
and though the words
are the same
the river they float on
no longer empties into yours.

What a hoarse siren offers
you've known. The gravel
at the bottom of that voice
has rolled in place for years,
bits and pieces of promises

and lies, like phony jewels
tumbling in a kaleidoscope,
its rattle belying their
brilliant combinations.

2. That's All

In the luminous hour
when everything becomes clear,
unlike itself,
surrendering its strangeness
to the clairvoyant glow of alcohol
we read the label
and laugh
as we did years ago:

Wilson:
Regardless of price
no better whiskey
in the world.

Still we can afford no more.
Cheap rooms. Cheap whiskey.

What have you done with your years?

You haven't saved any I see, lighting one
from the end of another like cigarettes.

3. The Glass

The glass
travels in families,
handed down,
sometimes filled
to the brim,
sometimes bone-dry
for generations:
yours now.

If it smashes
at midnight
against a wall,
or rolls off the counter
and shatters on the floor,
by morning
it will be whole again,
washed and rinsed
and standing by the sink.

Glass comes from sand,
sand from rocks
worn down, rock
that is the molten core
of stars, out of dust
and gas compressed.
You hold it in your hands,
remembering the wine
in which you nearly drowned,
and bless the emptiness
that fills you now.

PAPERWEIGHT

Everywhere,
defeated beauty:
in old pines,
toothless
against the sky
brand new each day;
in rivulets
running in the grooves
of the stones,
eroding the banks
of their lettering,
till they belong
to no one again,
names called out
to no reply
over crackling P.A. systems,
disembodied sound
that floats until it's hoarse
and breaking up
like fireworks
crumbled
on the velvet sky.
In the longing
that loses its way . . .
A vein drags
these words to light,
like nets
set out to dry,
stretched across the rocks
for mending,
then forgotten,
the sea–smell

blowing off,
the hand-tied knots
undone, tons of cold
green water pushing up,
full of bubbles
like this glass
paperweight
on the yard-sale table.

UNFINISHED POEMS

Is it sweat grown sweet from age
that draws you back
to undo this stack of dog-eared
yellow sheets, or some other
message seen in the stains
of coffee cups, glasses,
even burns that give off
faint smoke like talk that lingers
in the hair, the clothes,
the wallpaper of a room
your key no longer fits?

They are like ships in bottles
and old sealed watches,
and the bubbles in antique glass
that scientists seek
for samples of the air back then.

The finished ones are closed,
and emit no odors, tastes, or even noise,
but these bring along atmospheres
because they've been left open
and the air still flows through them.

Though they will probably never
get any better, or improve
enough to meet the light,
you read between the lines:
a chair, a desk, the room, the life.

In their erasures, blanks,
and crossed-out words,
endings that trail off,
in their breathlessness
and sputtering out . . .
their gaps
like coming up for air
from old and unremembered depths.

PUBLICATION

How small the words seem,
that were so large
in my head,
filling it for days;
moving them
took all my strength;
now they are light and airy,
half not there, like us,
like everything:
mostly empty space
between particles.
I shouldn't be surprised
the winter's work looks
so puny on the page.
Yet, here and there,
it sparkles a little,
inversely:
the colors reversed,
as on a blacktop roof,
the first flakes sticking,
their sound, their voice
not loud, but steady
whispering, mildly
stinging, beginning
the drifts that will cover us.

FORGIVE ME

Forgive me
for making a choice
between you and the force
that undermines my life
like a magnet pulling in
the wrong direction,
a choice that led me to the place
fear puts in us just as a test.
I know now what
I was doing then,
trying to create,
like men on streetcorners
who invent a language
that goes around the world,
something out of nothing:
the sum of my life to that point.
It looks foolish now, doomed
as someone trying to start
a fire from wet straw,
but then it was the only way.
I call it choice
to sound like
I control these bones,
the armature of pain
I know is mine.

POEM

Projected on the wall of heaven
the lights of an empty house
where someone used to sit
and write and read
deep into the nights
left unfilled like the black pages
at the end of a scrapbook . . .
Love was a storm, or star
up close, that stalled,
its matter churning,
burnt or sodden at the core,
edges fizzled and folded,
as flowers fold at night,
retreating from the bright darkness,
into the cave of an unlit heart.

WHEN THE AIR RUSHES IN

When the air rushes in
where we have been
and our absence is everywhere;
when the sky full of insects and birds
fills up the space where we stood
and a hummingbird stalls in your heart
and a crown of bees circles my head;
and when the grass pushes back
the last trace of this weight
and our footsteps climb with the dew;
may these words remember us,
when our breaths have blown away
and our names have turned to stone.

ON BREAKING A CHAIN LETTER

To Louise Glück

Let it end with me,
"this little prayer"
that has been around the world
nine times and has brought good luck
in the form of seven thousand dollars
to an American officer and sixty thousand
to Don Elliot, who lost it because
he broke the chain, and death
to Gen. Welsh in the Philippines
six days after he failed to send it on:
Let it end with me
so all my future disasters
can be explained.

POEM

In the "real world"—
I've been saying that
all my life, as if we
live protected from
the noise and action
outside. The puzzle
is how can we be
here and not-here,
feel and think as if
they were trains on
two different tracks?

If we are at the feet of,
the base of, that for which
our names shine,
why are there shadows
in the way, causing one
to think it's here, another
to see it where the other
says it used to be?

An awning flaps in the city
blue as the day-after sky
when the storm has moved
over Nova Scotia; a pen rests
beside a column of numbers,
holding up what?

A VOICE

"After the world is over,
and you catch your breath
that was so long tangled
up in limbs and wires,
and you're free
of those encumbrances
that held you back,
come to me."

"When you have closed your eyes
and then reopened them,
you'll see,
as from a plane window,
the world,
with its clever marquetry.
But this time
your reluctance
and disdain
doesn't hinder you,
you won't need to re-enter
that body, which belongs
down there. Stay here,
among clouds, discarded
shadows, emptied
breaths of the world,
where all its music flies.
Come to me."

Said a voice
between words
where nothing was;

just blank waking,
read only by fingers
feeling for feeling.

AFTER THE CALL

What is beyond all rooms and hours,
what they explode to show:
something standing in the doorway
that was not there a moment ago,
or the day before, but that will be there
forever now, on a level with the call,
and the voice it was in, your home already,
more than the words that were used,
the tone, the toll of a bell the heart answers.

TIGHTROPE

One end is tied in my heart,
this voice that goes out
past my body, well past
my line of sight, places
I've never been,
arcades and alleys,
in fog and sun,
over dark fields turning light,
over water rushing,
into winter, into rooms. . . .
Where the other end is tied
I have no idea, I only feel it,
perhaps in another heart—
I walk toward it.

BRIGHT SHADOW

Bright shadow
at dusk,
when others are reduced,
and sidewalks give off
waves of sadness . . .

Of a ghost
only the eyes
and smile remain,
after the face has crawled away.

I leave you flowers
(the vase is wrong):
heads on a platter
glowing, voices
of friends in the dark.

POEM

You who are carrying this book
down a dark hall
through flashing rooms
of subway cars,
hold it tight
like a statue
with a marble symbol
of undiscovered truth.
One day you will call me
the way I called them,
and they called theirs:
a rope ladder going back,
frayed and swaying,
and though the time
isn't at hand,
I have already answered.

LAST ENTRY

Who will read all this?
A thought with claws!
My friend
across the world
has written three great books
that sit unbound,
unbroken on his shelf
and mine. And I have
these tumbling words
that didn't have the sense
to stay unmade,
but used my breath
to fuel their fire,
my clock, my running sand
to blot their ink,
and scatter black
and blue and purple grains
the way sand paintings
always end, a rainbow
dispelled by hand,
and join chalky faces
from the sidewalk
risen as a prayer
to whoever listens
to the sea of words
that's always weeping,
asking, and finding
answers in an echo.

ACKNOWLEDGMENTS

The author wishes to thank the National Endowment for the Arts, the Massachusetts Council on the Arts, the Fine Arts Work Center in Provincetown, and the Corporation of Yaddo for support during the writing of this book.

Agni: "Poem" (Looking at this valley), "The Feather"

American Poetry Review: "After The Call," "Cerveteri," "The Glass," "Guard in a Cornfield," "Nothing's Changed," "A Night Like This," "Night's Silence," "Shadow Play," " Some Nights," "That's All," "Treasure Island," " Whose Requiem Is The Rain," "You Again"

The Ardis Anthology of New American Poetry: "Begin Here"

The Cape Cod Voice: "Fall," "Publication"

Cape & Islands: "Alba"

Crazyhorse: "Listening To Music"

The Greensboro Review: "The Somnambulist Blue"

Grand Street: "Little Elegy"

Harper's: "Indian Summer Garden Party"

The Iowa Review: "Inside Work"

The Missouri Review: "First Memory"

The New Yorker: "Working in Winter"

Ploughshares: "An Old Story"

Poetry: "Toy Soldiers"

Provincetown Arts: "For Mary Hackett"

Provincetown Poets: "On Breaking A Chain Letter"

Salt Hill: "Dusk"

The Seneca Review: "Something About The Stars," "Paper-
weight"

Shankpainter: "Hitchhiking," "Letter to an Ancestor,"
        "Lullaby"
The Sonora Review: "Poem" (Tired tonight)

Tikkun: "Notebook"

The Virginia Quarterly Review: "Black Leaves," "In Matera,"
        "The Impossible Bouquet," "On This Side," "Piero
        Manzoni," "Unfinished Poems," "The View"

Willow Springs: "Winter Dawn"

The Yale Review: "February"